MW00439070

Perversion
Tried to
Kill Me

John David Harris III

Copyright © 2019 by John David Harris III

All rights reserved. This book or any portion thereof may not be reproduced or used in any manner whatsoever without the express written permission of the publisher.

Dedication & Acknowledgments

I would first like to dedicate this book to *Holy Spirit*; this is literally because of *You*! I am grateful for what You've allowed me to write; You've inspired every word. You've led me into the truth of who I am and what it is that You've called me to do. Thank You for speaking to me in my darkest seasons when I could not see freedom for myself, let alone being used to free others. Thank You for helping me to carry ministry out of my misery.

To Araven, my beautiful mother, thank you for birthing me into the Earth at the perfect moment. Thank you for all of your many sacrifices, and for building me up to complete my kingdom assignment. To Aaneshea & A'zarya, my Sisters, I love you more than I'll ever be able to express! Thank you for always loving me and continuously affirming me. To my entire family, close friends, and loved ones, thank you for your continued support.

To My Spiritual Leaders, Pastors, and Mentors, thank you for your covering as well as support to release this book into the Earth.

To Pastor Jessica D. Williams, thank you for the initial nudge to write & completely finish this book.

Also, I would like to acknowledge the following for their services and time they've sown to make this assignment stress free for me! From the bottom of my heart, thank you!!

Daria Turner (Special effects make up)

Jerome Coverson - (Photography)

Justin Smith - (Graphics)

Yolanda Toney - (Editorial Service)

Champagne Mitchell - (Editorial Service)

Finally, to you, the reader, thank you for trusting me enough to walk with you through this journey of healing and deliverance. I dedicate this book to those who have been molested, raped, confused about their sexuality, addicted to pornography and/or masturbation, bullied, emotionally abused, broken, and rejected. I pray this book reaches you. Also, I must inform you that you will **NEVER** be the same after reading this book because I have released The Breaker (Jesus, our strong deliverer) on your behalf. He has been sent to rid you of your past. Therefore, I prophesy an *Isaiah 60:1* moment over your life:

"Rise and shine for your light has come, and the glory of the lord rises over you."

I speak to the Curse Breaker in you and say, "Rise!" To the Prophet in you, RISE. To the Deliverer in you, RISE. To the Teacher in you, RISE. To the Evangelist in you, RISE. To the Intercessor in you, RISE. To you who are called to miracles, RISE. To the free you, RISE. You will walk into the freedom of the Lord and out of the bondage of your yesterday. Fasten your seatbelt because here we go!

Table of Contents

Introduction

Have you ever felt like you were just walking through life with a target on your back? Have you been trapped into things you don't desire to do? Do you ever feel like you've been held hostage to the things you used to do? Can't seem to break free? I too have been in this predicament and what seemed to be just my sinful nature was actually a demonic curse that had attached itself to me. Its name is **PERVERSION**, and it **TRIED** to **KILL ME!** But I survived, and so will you!

The spirit of Perversion is a foul, demonic spirit that attaches to its prey, most of the time without the subject even knowing until it is too late to care. It is a very parasitic demon because it often attaches itself to individuals through demonic impartation, such as rape and/or molestation. The spirit of perversion also attaches itself through open portals, such as rejection and inward questioning of identity. This spirit loves to grow with you, so most of the time it sneaks in at an early age, and as you grow and develop, so does that spirit. You may not realize it, but everything you have been through in your life has probably nurtured the seed of perversion and made you more accessible to it. This spirit comes to twist and pervert

1

The people of God from their original design: morally, mentally, emotionally, spiritually, physically, financially, and sexually.

One of the first signs of perversion in the Bible occurs in *Genesis 3:1-7*. In this passage of scripture, a serpent was used to distort the vision of Adam and Eve.

The serpent used a momentary identity crisis to release the spirit of Perversion. Adam and Eve's perception and vision were perverted, which caused them not to see themselves as God had originally designed them. Just like Adam and Eve, most of us have had to cover up in things that were never designed for us because our vision has been shifted from purity to perversion.

I've come to realize that, like Eve, we all have had serpents whispering in our ears. Although your serpents did not tell you to eat a piece of forbidden fruit, whatever they told you was a lie. Therefore, it is time to take off the leaves and uncover the real YOU.

Chapter 1: Marked

Marked: being an object of attack.

T he spirit of Perversion snatched me up at an early age and its firm, relentless grip held on to me for most of my childhood and on into my adult life. After a night of literally wrestling with this spirit through prayer, God released to me my purpose in the Earth. My purpose is not to only expose that foul spirit, but to free those who have been held captive, tormented, tortured, and even violated by this spirit.

Now, realizing this heavy assignment did not come how many would expect. This assignment caused me years of pain, shame, and misery. Ashamedly, I spent years battling with this demonic spirit alone. I was addicted to masturbation and pornography, and I even dealt with strong desires to dabble in homosexuality. I probably watched a few thousand pornographic videos in my attempt to quench the thirst level of my demonic appetite for Perversion. Even after God released this VERY task to me, I still allowed Perversion to control my entire being. I wore Perversion like a second skin. Now, it was not something I was okay with at first, but once the door was opened, I was stuck. I felt that each time I gave in to this spirit, I was falling further and further from God's grace; I felt dirty. However, as I continued down this perverted path, it became a part of my nature. Looking back, it seemed to have been rooted in my DNA long before I realized it. I tried to be delivered multiple times, so I went to multiple altar calls, and I deleted resources that kept me from looking up pornography. In addition, I made personal declarations that I was not gay, and I tried a few more useless tactics. Of course, I did not understand then that to gain true, real, and pure deliverance, I first had to acknowledge the root cause of these actions. As I began to dig deeper and to pull the bandages off wounds I never truly dealt with, I realized that Perversion was not just something I had picked up, but it was a generational curse that was passed through my bloodline. Unknowingly, it had already engraved itself into my DNA; it was just waiting for me to turn off its dormancy.

I know for a fact that Perversion had marked me long before my birth. At the age of eight, I was molested by an older male, and from that moment, Perversion gained a deep foothold in my life. From then until I was twenty-one years old, Perversion took over my life and consistently tormented my mind. Little did I know, it would affect all my future relationships and friendships. I never could have imagined that it would break down my confidence and self-esteem, and even distort my sexuality. At the time of the molestation, I did not fully comprehend much of what happened, so I never discussed or addressed what had taken place. Suddenly, I was seventeen years old and in the fight for my life. I started beating myself up trying to figure out how I got to such a dark place. How did I, a worship leader and minister in my local church, end up here? Why was I masturbating at least three to four times a day, watching pornography for hours, looking at pictures, and imagining what it would be like to be with a guy? I was lost, and in complete ruin. So, God walked me through a series of processes to gain my freedom. It was and, at times, still is a FIGHT; however, I promised God and myself that I would not die at the hands of Perversion and that when I was set free, I would deliver entire generations for His glory. As a result, here I am; a survivor. Because I survived and annihilated the spirit of Perversion, you can and will too!

Declare This: <u>I WILL NOT DIE HERE!!!</u> I do not care who or where you are in your walk and journey to deliverance. This is my promise to you: If you fight, you WILL NOT DIE HERE!!!

I come now in the power of the Holy Spirit to serve this wicked enemy from Hell its eviction notice from YOUR life.

I declare even now as you are reading this book that the Spirit of the only LIVING God will come and invade your homes, cars, minds, and any other place the enemy has deposited seeds of perversion. I prophesy that those seeds will NO longer yield fruit, and every root of

5

perversion must be exposed now in Jesus' name. AMEN!

My desire is to walk with you through your deliverance process. In order to move forward, we must first back track to find out the *how:* How did you get to where you are today? Spirits of this nature (i.e. Perversion) do not just show up. First, you are exposed to them; then, you experience them, and lastly you accept them. I believe you are just pages away from experiencing a lasting deliverance, so let's jump right in.

Romans 10: 9-10 (NLT)

"9 If you declare with your mouth, "Jesus is Lord", and believe in your heart that God raised him from the dead, you will be saved. 10 For it is with your heart that you believe and are justified, and it is with your mouth that you profess your faith and are saved."

> ➢ **Do you believe in your heart and confess with your mouth "Jesus is Lord"?**

> ➢ **Do you believe God raised Him from the dead?**

> ➢ **Do you believe that one day He is coming back for you?**

If you answered **YES** to the following questions, you have just accepted salvation!

Congratulations on completing the very first step to deliverance: SALVATION! Yes, it's really that easy. However, without receiving salvation, we give God limited access to us, and we limit what we allow Him to do in us. Now that we have that out of the way, let's get to the workbook!

PTTKM Workbook Chapter 1 - Expose the Roots

Deliverance - the action of being rescued or set free.

The initial job of anyone who wants to be delivered from anything is to first realize that you are in bondage. You must then decide whether you want to be free or if you are comfortable where you are.

I want to start the opening to this workbook by asking you a simple, but very real question. Are you ready for deliverance? While this may seem like a weird question to ask, it is a valid one. Often time, we desire to be delivered from the act, rather than the root of the issue and the spirits that attach themselves to us as a result, This is how we find ourselves back to where we started because we truly were not ready. So again, are you ready for true deliverance? Are you ready to release the root?

Yes_____ No_____

1. When did you first notice that perversion or sexual immorality had entered your life? What was the very first seed or open door? Remember honesty breeds deliverance.

_____

_____

_____

2. A *generational curse* is a sinful or shameful cycle that passes through one's bloodline like a family heirloom, except it is spiritual. It can manifest as repetitive decisions and/or addictions.

What generational curses have you found yourself bound to?

_____

_____

_____

_____

3. What does deliverance mean to you?

_____

_____

_____

4. What are your expectations, as it pertains to this book? What forms of perversion are you desiring to be freed from?

_____

_____

_____

Strategic Prayer - Marked Prayer

Father, I thank You for saving me and giving me the opportunity to know You. Thank You for the blood of Jesus. Thank You for your sacrifice. Thank You for always giving me a way of escape! Father forgive me for any sinful acts I have committed and/or have been forced into. I ask that You wash me whiter than snow. Make me cleaner than I have ever been. Create in me a clean heart and give me a right spirit. Remove any demonic debris from my mind, body, and soul. As I take this journey through deliverance, search my heart and reveal to me anything that isn't pleasing to You. Remove me from the enemy's grip and strip me of anything that gives Satan a foothold in my life. Father, even now, cleanse my bloodline. I come now in the name of Jesus asking You to destroy and burn with fire EVERY generational curse that has held my bloodline and I captive. Father interrupt every single demonic snare, plot, and plan of the enemy for my life. Pluck out and uproot perversion, seeds of perversion, and any ungodly thing that has tried to spring up in my life. I decree that the curse is broken. I call every generational curse to the grave; I declare Perversion will see neither me nor my family anymore; not now, not ever! Its power is destroyed. I dismantle its reign over my life. Father, as I begin to dig even deeper to release Your healing for my life, I thank You that torment will NOT overtake my mind. Thank You that shame will not be my portion. Thank You that there is freedom in my transparency; thank You that your word says

10

in John 8:36: **"So if the son sets you free you will be free indeed."** The blood of Jesus makes me free: free from shame, guilt, addictions, and anything else that could possibly be thrown at me. I thank You for being my protector, and the enemy will not be able to retaliate against me nor my family because You've established a hedge of protection all about me. Freedom will not just be an appearance, but it will be my resting place in Jesus' name. AMEN!!!

Chapter 2: Sought After

Roots: the basic cause, source, or origin of something.

I began to take a deeper look into the WHY of my situation. I realized that, all along, it was a plan of the enemy. A plan to kill me; a plan to suffocate me in rejection and wrap it up in perversion. I originally misdiagnosed the root of my problem. I thought, initially, that it was simply perversion and sexual immorality. All the while, the true killer was rejection. Rejection drove me right into the welcoming arms of perversion, and perversion was patiently waiting to choke every ounce of life out of me. I initially encountered rejection when my parents divorced. I was too young to understand what had taken place. As I got older, I would reach out to my dad and not be able to reach him- physically or even just over the phone. As a result, I automatically labeled it as being unwanted or unloved by him. It was the first seed of rejection ever planted within my soul. Meanwhile, those seeds that were planted began to be watered by my peers during my elementary school years. I was the chubby kid in physical education (P.E.) who was never selected to play with the other kids. If I did get picked, it was only because I was the last option.

Even though my mom showed much love and affection and created a loving atmosphere at home, that did not stop the verbal abuse I received elsewhere.

Along with being left out at and getting picked on at school, I was also being called cruel names. I would often hear that I looked like a girl. I was told that I should have been born a girl and that I didn't look like a boy. This caused me to see myself as fat, ugly, and just big, which were some of the words that were spoken over me. Unfortunately, I began to think maybe I should have been a girl. I felt unimportant, unwanted, and unneeded. From that moment on, I accepted each word that people said I was, and I wore those words like a new outfit. It was at that moment that MY IDENTITY was ripped from me. One day when I got home from school, I went into the bathroom and just stared at myself in the mirror, and I broke down. I cried for almost an hour because I started to see myself the way others said I was. For the first time, every flaw about me was visible, so I eventually developed self-hate. This was the second big appearance of perversion in my life; the first was molestation which happened right around this same time. This was an appearance of perversion because I no longer saw myself as God saw me. It was like Rejection and Perversion had teamed up, and they started creating and cultivating a home in me. I then began having suicidal thoughts. Sadly, I was not even in middle school yet. But I was already debating if death would be better than the misery I had faced from day to day.

About two years later, one of the most humiliating incidents in my life occurred when I approached a girl who I had a crush on. I gathered all the courage I possibly could to ask her to be my girlfriend. I wrote her a letter because writing letters during that time was how we reached out to a love interest. The letter stated, "If you want to be my girlfriend, check yes or no." To my surprise, she showed the letter to the entire class, and they all laughed at me; she then threw the letter away. This act of rejection had unleashed new levels of terror in my life. Not only had I been molested by an older man, but I then had been bullied, left out, and repeatedly told I looked like a girl. I was then publicly humiliated by someone I admired. That moment of rejection watered seeds that had been planted earlier, and the roots of those seeds began to spread out in me. I was in ELEMENTARY school when I started thinking: *Well, maybe since girls don't like me, I'm supposed to be with boys. They say I look like a girl anyway.* This thought was sketched in my mind at a very young age. Soon after the thought went away, I didn't think much of it for a while.

Later, in seventh grade, I was exposed to same sex pornography, and something in me seemed to like it. When it was first presented to me, I pretended as if I did not want to see it, but it seemed familiar, and I had a burning desire to see it again. I just did not have the courage to look that

14

up myself. In the eighth grade, I decided to watch pornography for the first time on my own, so I quietly went into the bathroom, and I locked the door and watched it extremely carefully. While watching, I began to masturbate, and it was the best feeling ever. However, this was the very first time I had opened the door of pornography and masturbation for myself. I just knew before I could even exit off the website that God was going to take my life. I felt like everyone knew what I had just done. I went to church that night, I cried out for forgiveness, and I told God I would not ever do it again. One year later, I started high school, and I must admit that ninth grade was hard for me, much like my previous school experiences. I felt alone, as if I was in high school by myself. I did not know anyone, and I was an overweight teenager who was an easy target for bullying.

As a result of constant bullying, I was now introduced to the spirit of depression, which literally consumed my entire being. I no longer knew what joy was, and I was spiritually in a blur. In the back of my mind, I knew God was always with me, but my present state convinced me that He was nowhere around; so, I operated as such. I remember sitting in math class, and the only equation I was trying to solve was how I was going to kill myself. As tears ran down my face, I remember thinking: *God, I just can't do this* any*more.* I felt like life had become unbearable. I had no stress reliever, no way to cope with how I felt, and I had never really been one to talk much about my feelings. I would much rather try to find my own solution and boy did I find one.

In my search for a way to be okay, I became reacquainted with the then dormant spirit of Perversion that was quietly resting in me. This time, it was bred out of loneliness, depression, and curiosity. High school was a different atmosphere, there was an aroma of promiscuity that filled each hallway. I would hear people discuss the benefits of indulging in their personal temptations. It seemed to work for everyone else. So, I decided I would give it a shot again. One day after school, I went home, walked in the bathroom, locked the door behind me, and looked up pictures of naked women. It was cool for the moment; however, it was not enough, so I moved on to videos. I remember the anxiety I felt looking at my phone. Using my search engine, I typed in *porn*, and a variety of websites, pictures, and videos popped up. I watched cautiously, in fear of being caught. I then proceeded to masturbate; this was my second time ever. Instantly, I felt like a door that I had no business touching had just been opened. However, yet again it was the best feeling I had ever had. Then suddenly, I was met with a sorrow I could never explain. I knew it was wrong because I felt so dirty and disgusting, but it was not as bad as the first time I felt it. I knew what I had done was wrong. Therefore, I repented and promised God that I would never do it again, and I meant every word…until the irresistible desire came back. Just the mere thought of the overwhelming sensation of acceptance and pleasure I felt made me do it again, and I repented again. This was wrong, and I knew it, but for some reason it felt so good. This was way deeper than just a sexual desire. This helped me cope with emotional issues I had faced all my life. It was like I had finally found a cure to my depression.

Pornography allowed me to escape reality. All I had to focus on was this beautiful naked woman on the screen. How I felt about myself in this moment did not matter. Therefore, I continued to masturbate and watch pornography, and each time I started to feel a little less sorry about it. Slowly, I went from masturbating once a month, to once every two weeks, to once a week, then once every three days, to once every other day. The next thing I knew I was masturbating three to four times a day. I loved this feeling; it was my favorite place to be, so I started to just accept it. I figured it was helpful, as it was what I needed. I was always looking for a cure, and finally I had found one. Or, so I thought.

PTTKM Workbook Chapter 2 - Triggers

1. Have you experienced identity issues? Have you accepted and received word curses spoken over you? Has rejection made you feel unwanted?

   Have you found and used ungodly coping mechanisms that seem to satisfy and numb you?

   _____

   _____

   _____

   _____

2. Who rejected you? Who made you feel like you weren't good enough? What have people spoken over you that pushed you into the welcoming arms of perversion?

   Give incidents and time frames in which the incident or incidents occurred.

   _____

   _____

   _____

   _____

   _____

   _____

3. At this very moment, STOP!!! Forgive whomever or whatever you feel pushed you to this place. Often, the root or reason you dealt with perversion has nothing to do with you, but more so with the person or thing that hurt you.

You may have been rejected or molested, raped, abused verbally, physically, or even mentally. Whatever it is, you must release it NOW!!!

Your deliverance depends solely on your power to release. Write a letter of forgiveness and release the thing that you have no desire to speak of.

_____

_____

_____

_____

_____

_____

_____

_____

_____

_____

_____

Strategic Prayer - Revealing and Removing Roots

Father, I thank You for my identity, and though the enemy has used triggers and deep roots from my past and opened doors to push ME outside of who You declared I was, I thank you for restoration. Just as the father restored the prodigal son to who he was called to be in **Luke 15**, I thank You because You are restoring me. Thank You for removing humiliation from my life; thank You for breaking Rejection off of me. I am NOT in the middle of an identity crisis. Thank You that I am loved by You, so I will no longer seek love in any other place. I ask that You forgive me for searching for a greater love than Yours. Your love affirms me; Your love highly esteems me, and Your love lifts me. I find confidence in me because of You; there is no love like Yours in ALL the earth. I thank You for grace. Even when I used supplements to replace Your love, You stayed right there and waited for me. You have patiently waited. THANK YOU!!! Even now, You are still waiting for me. You are a long-suffering God (Exodus 34:6) Thank You for not giving up on me; thank You for never letting me go. Thank You for Your lavish love toward me. You are the God who removes low self-esteem. Your word announces that I am fearfully and wonderfully made. You took Your time with me. Jeremiah 1:5 decrees that You knew me before You formed me in my mother's womb, and for that I say thank You. You see me as priceless and as one of a kind. Nothing and no one will keep me from being who

You say I am. Thank You that at the name of Jesus every demonic entity must bow. Thank You, Jesus, that my past no longer binds me. I am released to be who You say I am. Now Father remove every word curse that has kept me bound in cycles and break every chain that the enemy has wrapped around my neck to hold me hostage to what has been comfortable and familiar. I will dive into Your freedom for my life. I thank You that freedom will not be an appearance, but it will be my resting place in Jesus' name. AMEN!!!

Chapter 3: Captured

Captured: to be taken into one's possession or control by force.

Captured… Yep, I was spiritually lost, physically out of control, and mentally numb. It was like being in a sea of perversion and sexual immorality, and I was no longer floating or enjoying the swim. I was drowning deeper and deeper in my secret sin. It was not fun anymore. I no longer had a choice. I would wake up out of my sleep masturbating; sexual dreams and desires overtook my sleep and began to torment my mind. I would spend several hours at a time looking up pictures of naked women and men. There were nights I could not sleep without masturbating at least once. I became blind; it was like I could not see past my next opportunity to do it all over again. I was now chained to this. Any alone time I had was used for masturbation and pornography. My free time was devoted to this life-threatening disease which had taken over my mind completely. If I was not at school, work, or church, I was probably somewhere watching pornography and masturbating. It got so bad that when I did not have my phone or pornography, I would masturbate just to do it. Pictures, ideas, and fantasies consistently filled my mind; the more I imagined, the more things I looked up. I had probably watched almost every kind of pornographic film possible. In this lost place was where all the seeds of both rejection and perversion came together and began to swallow me up. I started watching same sex pornography, considering whether1 I was cut out for the homosexual lifestyle. It was not purely because of attraction, but mainly because I had never felt love on a romantic level or ever felt wanted by a female. I remember thinking back to when I was molested and thinking maybe that happened because that was the lifestyle I was meant to live.

Thoughts of how any girl I had ever approached rejected me in some way, or how whenever I was in public, I would be mistaken for a woman played on my emotions for a long time. I became anxious when meeting new people because I did not want to hear "ma'am" or get confused for a woman. I was tired of explaining myself. One of the most humiliating and identity-destroying experiences of my life was when I was at a church service, and this "prophet" called me out and said, "Sis, God said He's upgrading you; you're about to get a new hairdo, and He's about to change you." At that point, I was in complete and total shock and I was so embarrassed. The worst part was that the "prophet" then asked all the women in the church to come give me a hug. The way it all happened had me completely stuck and lost for words, so much so that I could not think straight or move to walk out.

Uncomfortably, I was surrounded by a crowd of women, and they all walked up to me saying things like: "You're beautiful Baby Girl," and "God loves you Sis." All I could do was cry, and they thought that this "prophet" was effective. Little did they know, this was the most embarrassing moment of my entire existence. I found one of the leaders of the service and I told her, "He called me a woman; I'm male." Her response was, "Were you born a woman or a man?" That by far was the most devastating event to ever take place in my life. All these things pushed me to contemplate the idea of being with a male. I thought about that idea for years; the thoughts of being accepted or just to be wanted snatched me up. The scary thing about perversion is once you open yourself up to one realm, multiple doors are opened. By that time, I was not only addicted to pornography and masturbation, I was considering whether being "gay" was going to be my new norm. If there was anything I knew for certain, I knew this was not God. Everything in me knew this was not His plan for my life. I could not believe that I was at a point where I considered a homosexual lifestyle. I knew for certain that perversion had taken me too far. I began battling with homosexual thoughts and decided to just dismiss them. However, I continued in what I was comfortable in. Uncomfortably, I had begun trying to come back to my senses. **Jeremiah 3:14** declares, "The Lord is married to the backsliders." These words held true for me.

One day as I was doing my usual pornography and masturbation session, God spoke to me and proclaimed,

"This very thing you're going through will minister to others; you will write about this."

In that moment, I became completely overwhelmed. I could not fathom that God had just spoken to me in the middle of me watching pornography and masturbating. My thoughts were: *God, you care THIS much about me to not wait until I finish my mess, but right in the thick of it, prophesy over my life?* He did not wait until I was delivered, but He started giving me strategy even then on how I would flip my mess into His message. That was 2015. Even with that specific word from God, the battle did not end there, and after much thought, I later decided to download gay dating apps. I told God since no females wanted me, this is what I was going to do. I then started communicating with men. I decided it was who I was always meant to be. I was destined for this lifestyle. It was always after me, so I stopped running from it and instead, pursued it. I had even planned to meet up with one guy. I no longer desired to be kept by God. I intentionally stepped out of the ark of safety. I was consumed, and I wanted to be. I tried my hardest to live in that lifestyle, and it just did not happen. God blocked and arrested my agenda. My spirit began to travail regardless of whether I desired it to do so or not. It was almost as if I had no choice but to listen to Holy Spirit. I knew that day I did not want to continue pursuing a lifestyle the enemy designed to capture and kill me with. I was ready to break out of the prison I had been trapped in all my life, and I did.

The journey was not easy, and freedom is not absolutely free. You can and you will break out. I prophesy that even as you are reading this that you will be troubled in your spirit for change. This is your word to shake you out of your captured place. This is a good moment to just pause and surrender.

Journal Entry

Have you answered the cry of your spirit? What is your spirit man saying? No matter who you are or what you have done, you have a spirit, and it speaks. I think it is time you listen. ***Don't just skip past this part, but actually focus to hear what your spirit man has to say to you.*** *

_____

_____

_____

_____

_____

_____

_____

_____

_____

_____

_____

Strategic Prayer for Freedom - Captured Place

Father, I surrender right NOW!!! I lay all of the baggage I've carried at Your feet, and I will never desire to pick it up again. Please forgive me for taking Your place, for making myself an idol, and for catering to my will and fleshly desires. Deliver me; deliver me from the captured place I've resided in for so long. I believe You to be the God who restores. So, I declare now in the name of Jesus that I'm getting my mind back, and every impure, demonically charged thought of the enemy is evicted. Father destroy any unholy sexual thoughts, desires, and visuals; may they be removed now in the mighty name of Jesus. Thank You for mental and spiritual sobriety. I will guard my spirit and my mind. Thank You for being a refuge, even when thoughts and desires try to creep in my mind late in the midnight hour. Thank You for freeing me from all addictions and spiritual prisons that have held me hostage. I declare I will sleep at night; I declare un-Godly desires will not haunt and torment me. I pray that every perverse spirit that arises in my dwelling place will be sent to dry places. I release angels to watch over me. Father, I give You back Your rightful place in my life. You belong first, and You will be the first thought I have in the morning and last thought before I sleep. Thank You for not giving up on me, even when I continued to lounge in my mess. Thank You for shaking me out of this captured state of mind and spirit. Thank You for freedom. I am no longer captive, and I am no longer the victim. The blood of Jesus has covered me. I am stained and submerged in the blood, and when the enemy comes to look for me, he won't find me because I am hidden in You! I have been awakened, and I will arise to do and be all that You have called me to do and be. Even now, Father consume that which desires to consume me in Jesus' name. Thank You that every dysfunctional place in my life is being destroyed.

Thank You that as I pray this prayer, demons are running into hiding because You are releasing strategy to me and not only will I be free, but I will remain free! Holy Spirit, I welcome You to dwell in every area of my life and reveal any area that You're not willing to be a part of, and I will remove it. I announce that freedom will not be an appearance, but it will be my resting place in Jesus' name. AMEN!!!

Chapter 4: Breakout

Breakout: a forcible escape, typically from prison.

The breakout point is the crossroads of your deliverance. In this place, you must decide that you CANNOT go back, and it may even seem like you are so far from where you know you should be. This is the place where most of you are now or will soon be. You know what you have been dabbling in is wrong, and you are tired and ready for freedom. That is probably why you are reading this book now. However, you must know that this place is NOT for wimps. In this season of your life, it will require a will to fight. For me, this was one of the hardest parts of deliverance because I knew for sure there was no way I was going back. While that fact remained, my desire to please my flesh was still there, as well. This place literally takes the strategy of the Lord.

This was such a difficult part for me because I was in a place where I went from masturbating three to four times a day to completely stopping because I was so desperate to be free, but I had no strategy and that made this almost impossible. It then became a battle of what my spirit knew I needed to do and what my flesh thought it could handle. This became a test of my limits and what I could and could not take. Quite naturally, this was a season of withdrawal from what was comfortable. Let's be practical; this is something I was used to doing daily. When I started this process of deliverance, I stopped the act for about a week, and it was hard, so for that week I was able to find ways or routes to avoid it, and that next week my flesh came back so strong that it seemed like I had never started the journey to deliverance. I was relying more on my desire for freedom instead of the keeping power of Jesus. So I had to ask God for strategy to get free. For me, it took more than an altar call.

I quickly learned that to be and to stay delivered, it would take a fresh "yes" every single day. Often time, we believe that we will be delivered based on the initial decision to be free; however, an initial decision to be free is timed, which is why you must make that decision every single day of your life. This was my issue. I was eager to be free, but I wanted to span my entire deliverance journey off one "yes". I ignored the fact that yesterday's "yes" gets old. You will quickly learn that the process is daily, and you grow in it over time. **You must give God a fresh "yes" every single day.**

As I received strategy from the Lord, I slowed down a lot, and I cut it to a minimum. There were times I just gave in, but there were also times I pleaded with God for my life. I remember going to altar calls for deliverance and walking away with what I thought was temporary deliverance, and I was discouraged. I felt like it should have just been over with by now, but it simply just does not work like that. You do not usually become entangled in sin overnight, so you cannot always expect to be freed from it overnight; there must be a daily untangling.

The deliverance process may not be overnight, and that is okay because we are seeking progression and not perfection. There were times I failed and still masturbated in my breakout season, but it was not comfortable, and I was not okay with it. I enjoyed getting this feeling back because I longed to feel bad about what I had been doing, and I knew conviction would continue to breed my deliverance. Even in this state, I could see the shore of my deliverance. You must see yourself free even before freedom comes. Eventually, I decreased from masturbating four times a day to once every three days and from every three days to once every week and from once every week to once every two weeks and from once every two weeks to once every month. Finally, I was able to go months without falling. Complete freedom is not only possible, but realistic and obtainable. I must admit that it will continue to be a process. I have come to learn that in this process you will have many shortcomings, but falling into a pit and jumping into a pit are two totally different things. God allowed me to walk out my deliverance in two parts, and it has been extremely helpful in my continued success on the journey of deliverance.

Part I: Getting Free from the Stuck Place

Part II: Staying Free

Now that we understand it is a journey and a process, let's move into the practicalities of freedom, which involve a walking out of strategy. At this point in your deliverance, you stop using defense, and you use offense because you are no longer waiting for the enemy's next move. You set boundaries. You must draw a line in the sand. You must make demands. In this season, I was completely angry at the enemy and decided not to allow him to sabotage my life anymore. You must be intentional about EVERYTHING. Now my strategy and your strategy will differ a little, but ask God for specific guidance, and He WILL help you develop a tailor-made strategy. As for me, I became meticulous about every detail of my life. I stopped listening to any music other than worship music. I believe that music is simply the soundtrack to life, and no matter what you are doing there is a song and a sound that will influence you. From then until now, I very rarely listen to anything else. People may call you boring, but you must understand what you do is for YOU. Nobody needs you to be free like you need you to be free. I've learned to allow worship to impact every aspect of my life at every moment. No matter where I am, I try my best to continually be in God's presence because my flesh and the Father obviously cannot dwell together. I guarded the television shows I watched; I learned that I could not entertain shows or movies with a bunch of sex in them. While you may be thinking that sex is in every show, maybe you should not be watching television until you can find things that fit your specific season. These are decisions I made daily to keep my vow with the Lord fresh every day. You must learn to not put yourself in situations where your flesh will rise. No matter what you are doing, you are always creating an atmosphere, either for purity or perversion, and they do not dwell together. It is vital that you also watch the company you keep, because they will either push you to freedom or provoke you to continue in perversion. Nevertheless, you must be transparent, and you cannot keep this battle that you are fighting to yourself. Accountability partners are mandatory! You need someone who knows your good, bad, and outright disgusting. Remember, this is a practical process just as much as it is a spiritual one! Therefore, you must find practical solutions. After you leave the altar call, these are the strategies you must use! We'll talk more about strategies later, but for now let's jump into the workbook portion of chapter 4.

PTTKM Workbook Chapter 4 – Breakout

1. What is your biggest personal hindrance from experiencing the freedom of the Lord?

_____

_____

_____

2. What does **practical** deliverance mean to you?

_____

_____

_____

Strategic Prayer – The Breakout Prayer

Father, I thank You for power! Power to break out of every cage and demonic prison that I have been held in. Thank You for power to break out of every chain and fetter. I declare now that I am rising, and I am walking in the authority that you gave me, authority to speak to my mind and declare deliverance, authority to speak over my spirit and the desires of my flesh. I declare now that practicality is my portion, and I will use practical solutions to guard my spirit. I declare that every unholy spirit is being removed, even as I pray this prayer. Every unrighteous thought and visual is being uprooted even now. I WILL walk though this deliverance process with boldness and grace. I will be as a lion, and every time the enemy comes to eat of my flesh I will ROAR! My roar will send the enemy running. Thank You that I have been awakened to the reality of who I am. No longer will I be tormented. No longer will the enemy keep my mind. The enemy has no control or power over my actions. Every trap is destroyed. Every entry way that seducing spirits previously had in me has been SLAMMED SHUT!!! I announce that freedom will not be an appearance, but it will be my resting place in Jesus' name. AMEN!!!

Chapter 5: The Escape

The night before I began to write this chapter, I had a dream. In that dream, I was trapped in a huge fenced-in house with many other people, and we were all trying to escape, but for some reason we could not. After a while, many stopped, but I kept trying. I would break out of the house. As I would attempt to jump the fence, this device that was put in my leg would then send an unbearable wave of pain that would not stop until I got back into the house. It was almost like a shock collar. So, after another failed attempt, I ran back into the house, and I ended up back in the room with everyone who had been stuck in the house. As we sat there, the room became like a gas chamber, and gas was released from the ceiling. I found a shirt and a bottle of water, and I poured the water on the shirt and inhaled from there. I then laid down and pretended as if the gas had killed me because most of the others did not survive. Then the person who was doing all of this entered the room to make sure everyone was dead. He thought we were all dead! He walked out, so I attempted to escape again. As I was running to the fence, the device that was put in my leg started to shock me again. Before I could be seen, I ran back into the house and cut the device out of my leg. From that moment, I was able to escape because what had been keeping me there was now removed.

As I began to reflect on that dream, God revealed to me that the house was Perversion. I realized that the signal that kept making me run back to the house was just like how our flesh responds when we make the decision to run away from sexual immorality and pursue freedom. When you have been so accustomed to a lifestyle, your mind-soul will tell you there is no way you can be free, so you might as well go back to that house of bondage that you were comfortable in. Your flesh will even cry out for what you know you must escape from.

There is only one way to remove that signal, and that is to renew your mind:

Romans 12:2 (KJV) "And be not conformed to this world: but be ye transformed by the renewing of your mind, that ye may prove what is that good, and acceptable, and perfect, will of God."

Your mind CAN be transformed! One of the biggest parts of deliverance is having a mental shift. Once you shift your mind, your flesh has no choice but to follow.

Ephesians 4:22-24 (NLT) "Throw off your old sinful nature and your former way of life, which is corrupted by lust and deception. Instead, let the Spirit renew your thoughts and attitudes. Put on your new nature, created to be like God—truly righteous and holy."

40

*To "THROW OFF" means to make forcible movement to discard or cast off.

In the dream, I was able to break out of the house several times. Although I broke out of the house, it did not mean that I was not still on the property. Similar to how many of us have loosened the cuffs of perversion but have not taken them off! I escaped because I cut out the very device that kept pressuring me to return, and that takes desperation. In your life, you must do the same. In the dream, this device was behind my kneecap, and I had to cut my leg open, pull back my kneecap, and pull out the device. Can you imagine yourself pulling things off that have been rooted in you for years? It's painful, right? If you want to stop being forced to a place of return, you will do what it takes to get free! This is what it takes to fight against the wiles of the enemy.

Let's get something clear. Even though you have broken out of perversion (The House), it does not automatically mean you're no longer on the property. In this chapter, I will dive into the depth of strategy to flee from it and stay away. It is at this point where strategy and your desire to live meet. With that couple, you can escape anything, but you must RUN for your life. The last thing we want to do is partially break out of the system of perversion and not run away from or escape it completely. The reason that most of us continue to fall, slip, or even jump back into sexual sin is because we do not take the proper steps to completely escape, so we often experience temporary deliverance. Being free from the act is great, but you must be free totally from your will in order to experience limitless freedom.

James 4:7 (KJV) recommends: "Submit yourselves therefore to God. Resist the devil, and he will flee from you."

When it comes to resisting the devil, you must FIRST submit yourself before the Father. In order to submit before the Father, you must submit your WHOLE life. Often, we only want to submit the parts WE think He should have, so we experience partial deliverance since we partially submit. I believe if you want total deliverance, every agenda you have must be submitted to the will of the Father. You can only be tempted by what you desire. When you submit and relinquish your will to take on the will of the Father, your desires become His desires, so the enemy will have to flee because he no longer has real estate in your flesh. That is why the enemy has such a huge issue with us submitting to God because he knows he will lose property. I announce now that the enemy of your soul is experiencing MASS FORECLOSURE because The God of Angel Armies is taking back what belongs to Him.

Declare This: I break every demonic contract I have signed with my actions and desires. Father, forgive me, and destroy every agreement I had with Satan. He has no property here in Jesus'! Amen!!!

After you have submitted to God and started to take on His will for your life, you must then do what I like to call "creating a space." This is the part that happens when no one is around, but it is one of the most important parts.

Cultivating a place where God can dwell and live with you consistently so that you have continual communion is what causes the enemy to flee. You should be willing to create a physical place as well as a spiritual, emotional, and mental space for God to live.

Now let's talk strategy to ensure that your deliverance will have longevity:

Removing people from your process

1) It is not everyone's place to know what is going on. Negative people will hold you back from experiencing your full deliverance, so they will tell you that you are "doing too much", and you do not have to do "all that".

However, I am here to tell you that you must do all that, this, and more.

2) Remove friends who promote your continued journey in perversion and watch out for people who try and provoke you. I am sorry to tell you, but the road to deliverance becomes lonely. Everyone will not understand your process. If you are afraid of losing friends, you may never be able to experience complete freedom. You may be called the boring friend, but please

43

know that it is okay. For me, there are certain music genres and music artists I will not listen to because music usually initiates our actions. There will be a season in your deliverance where the only thing you listen to might be worship music, but you are not being weird or being too saved. You must guard your gates and what you allow in your spirit and mind. People who have dealt with perversion, specifically masturbation and pornography, just have an amazing imagination that comes with the territory. So, to shift the direction of your imagination you must shift what you are allowing to flow into your mind.

3) Release the negative word curses people have spoken over you. To release is to throw away, discard, and reject. Many people spoke over my sexuality and said what I was, what I should have been, and what it looked like I was. They judged how I walked and talked. Unfortunately, I allowed them and everything I had been through to shape my sexuality. As a result, I made the decision to be free based on what God desires for me. I walked out of homosexuality as soon as I took off the world's perception of me. I was no longer the word curses, molestation, or rejection that had been placed on me.

4) Release the negative perception of yourself. Release the word curses you have spoken over yourself.

5) Come to grips with the truth. No one can hold the truth

against you. Do not allow your former truth to control you. Do not let shame and condemnation choke you.

6) Take on God's perception of you. Allow God's thoughts concerning you to be the only facts that matter. Here is how our Father feels about you:

   • *1 Thessalonians 5:5 (NLT) affirms: "For you are all children of the light and of the day; we don't belong to darkness and night."*

(Your identity is a child of the light).

   • *Romans 8:38-39 (NLT) declares: "And I am convinced that nothing can ever separate us from God's love. Neither death nor life, neither angels nor demons, neither our fears for today nor our worries about tomorrow—not even the powers of hell can separate us from God's love.*

   39 No power in the sky above or in the earth below — indeed, nothing in all creation will ever be able to separate us from the love of God that is revealed in Christ Jesus our Lord."

(Nothing can separate you from your Father, for He sees you as being worth staying with. He'll never leave you nor forsake you. How amazing is that to know, that not even angels or demons can separate you from God! If you ever feel distance between you and your Father, it's because you moved, NOT Him).

- *1 Peter 2:9 (NLT) professes: "But you are not like that, for you are a chosen people. You are royal priests, a holy nation, God's very own possession. As a result, you can show others the goodness of God, for he called you out of the darkness into his wonderful light."*

(You are royalty, for you are a son! You live in the light).

Not gender-based but position-based

- *John 15:15-16 (NLT) assures: "I no longer call you slaves, because a master doesn't confide in his slaves.*

Now you are my friends, since I have told you everything the Father told me. 16 You didn't choose me. I chose you. I appointed you to go and produce lasting fruit, so that the Father will give you whatever you ask for, using my name."

(Jesus calls you His follower. **Friend**. Chosen).

- *Romans 8:17 (NIV) confirms: "Now if we are children, then we are heirs —heirs of God and co-heirs with Christ, if indeed we share in his sufferings in order that we may also share in his glory."*

(You are Heirs with Christ).

- *Matthew 5:13 (NIV) asserts: "You are the salt of the Earth."*

(You were sent to preserve the Earth).

YOU NEED ACCOUNTABILITY

1) You must first be accountable for yourself and your actions to God. *Romans 14:12 (KJV) states: "So then each one of us shall give account of himself to God."*

Be accountable to yourself. What standard are you holding yourself to?

2) You also need an accountability partner because you must have someone you can be extremely honest with and someone who will tell you the truth. You need someone who will not judge you. You should not have to worry about judgement, and do not receive everything they say as judgement. Transparency is a huge part of any deliverance process, especially for secret sexual sins. Therefore, your accountability partner should be someone you know is praying for you. This is not the time for a "misery loves company" type of situation.

Galatians 6:1-2 (KJV) recognizes: "Brethren, if a man be overtaken in a fault, ye which are spiritual, restore such a one in the spirit of meekness; considering

47

thyself, lest thou also be tempted. Bear ye one another's burdens, and so fulfill the law of Christ."

Hebrews 10:24-25 (KJV) notes: "And let us consider one another to provoke unto love and to good works: Not forsaking the assembling of ourselves together, as the manner of some is; but exhorting one another: and so much the more, as ye see the day approaching."

1 Thessalonians 5:11 (AMP) conveys: "Therefore encourage and comfort one another and build up one another, just as you are doing."

3) Be accountable to your leaders (for those apart of a church or Christian organization). Your leaders should know what it is you are facing, and they should cover your souls, so they can better assist you when they know what it is you have struggled with. They will not put you in compromising situations.

4) Being transparent with your family is important. You never know how your family could use your transparency; you could break the generational curse just by talking about it.

Purify Your Space

Your space could be your room, a certain part of your house, or even your car. Also, any space where you dealt territory to the enemy by operating in any form of perversion should be purified.

To purify this space, you need to:

- Repent.

- Ask God to remove the unclean spirits you released in your space. (You can find this prayer in chapter 7).

- Give that space to God. (Devote what belongs to you to God).

- Ask for the presence of God to fill your space. Ask God to release His sweet spirit in the room/space. (He will do it).

- Remove anything that provokes you to sin or reminds you of a season you know you should completely do away with.

- Get rid of any Erotic books and tools the enemy uses to keep you bound.

- Fill that space with things that remind you of the presence of God. For instance, I would often masturbate in my bedroom. I put a prayer shawl around the headboard, and when I would feel weak in my flesh, I would just reach my hand out and touch it, and immediately my flesh would subside. Every time I would touch, I would immediately feel strength come back to me. Be intentional about your deliverance. Distractions only free you momentarily, but Godly remedies increase the longevity of your freedom.

- Allow worship to consume this space.

- In this space, prayer is a MUST. The biggest way to overcome any ungodly desire is prayer, and it sounds stereotypical of me to say, I know. However, whatever you release in your space is what will dwell there. Remain strong and courageous during moments of weakness.

- *Ephesians 6:12 reveals: "For we wrestle not against flesh and blood, but against principalities, against powers, against the rulers of the darkness of this world, against spiritual wickedness in high places."*

We do not fight in the natural, but when we do fight, we do not fight fair. We automatically win. When you pray, know that your prayer is being heard, and then respond as such.

Purify Your Social Media

- Remove people who post content that is not conducive to your freedom.

- **DO NOT GET ON SOCIAL MEDIA IDLY!!!** I cannot tell you how many times I got onto social media in mere boredom to only end up on pornography websites because I saw something on social media that intrigued me sexually.

- I could not even look up fitness pages for a while because my motives were not pure, my desire was not to get in shape. I just wanted to see half-naked people. It takes this kind of honesty to release the next level of deliverance. Ask yourself a question: Why do I do what I do?

- There were times when I wanted to watch pornography or masturbate, but instead of just doing it, I would try and get motivation, so I would browse the internet until something aroused me. As a result, I would shoot straight to pornographic sites, which is what I wanted to do all along. I acted as if I was just living life, and humanity was getting the best of me, but truly I put myself in predicaments that would cause me to fall. Are your motives pure?

- Who you follow says a lot about you.

- Even while overcoming homosexuality, there are limits and measures that must be taken. Remove those who entice you. Flee from anything that keeps the door of perversion open in any area of your life, including social media.

Triggers

- You must learn what triggers your flesh into rising. Explain your triggers to those you do life with because they need to know how to prevent you from retreating to what you have been accustomed to.

51

- Counteract your triggers with the word of God. The word of God silences vain imagination, so do not be afraid to dive in.

- Be proactive concerning your flesh.

- Understand that just because you are triggered does not mean you have to allow your flesh to have its way. Manhandle your flesh and bring it under subjection.

JESUS!!!!!

The best kept secret is **JESUS**. Please know that His name is like having a loaded machine gun; it is not just something that sounds cool. The next time your flesh begins to act up I dare you to just shout the name Jesus with every fiber of your being! Watch what will happen! Every demon must back up. At the name of Jesus, Heaven and Earth and everything between must stand at attention. Do not underestimate His infinite power.

These strategies together should make reaching freedom so much easier. The key is consistency and combining every tool you have. When I began, my issue was using the keys that were comfortable and thinking I would get results. You must be intentional, and I pray you are ready for your escape because the escape is ready for you!

PTTKM Workbook Chapter 5 – The Escape

1) In what areas of your life can you create a space for God?

_____

_____

_____

2) Who are your accountability partners, and are they truly helpful? Can they speak to your future while understanding the depth of your past?

_____

_____

_____

3) Are there any relationships that you know are hindering your freedom? If so, what are you going to do about them?

_____

_____

_____

_____

_____

_____

4) What other strategies can you use to help you escape and stay free?

_____

_____

_____

5) How can you renew your mind daily?

_____

_____

_____

6) From the strategies listed above, which will be the easiest and most difficult for you to implement?

_____

_____

_____

Strategic Prayer – The Escape

Father, thank You that hell has lost its grip. It NO longer controls me, the moves I make, or the thoughts I think, nor can it control my appetite or desires. Thank You for a total mental shift. For Your word says in *Romans 12:2 (KJV):* *"And be not conformed to this world: but be ye transformed by the renewing of your mind, that ye may prove what is that good, and acceptable, and perfect, will of God."* Thank You for giving me strength for the renewing of my mind. I desire Your will for my life. Father, I pray that You will send me people after Your heart who will push and provoke my continued deliverance, and I ask that You remove everything that provokes me to perversion. I declare escape over my life, and I am grateful for the escape route that You have established in Your word. Thank You for strategy that releases freedom over my life. As I create a space for You, I ask that You remove every demonic and perverted spirit that I allowed in the space You have given me to govern. **I speak now under the power of the Holy Spirit, and I announce that every spirit of rejection, depression, and perversion is DISMISSED! Every portal and door I opened to perversion is SLAMMED SHUT! I have BROKEN ANY AGREEMENT I had with Rejection, Depression, and every form of perversion. THE CONTRACT HAS BEEN BROKEN!!! Devil, YOU NO LONGER HAVE A ROOM HERE!!! YOU CAME IN ONE WAY, BUT YOU WILL LEAVE IN SEVEN!!! (Deuteronomy 28:7).**

You are permitted to live here no longer in the matchless name of Jesus.

Holy Spirit, I welcome You back where You belong. I welcome back joy, peace, and love where they belong. Father let the aroma of Your presence fill this space. **FILL THIS SPACE! FILL THIS SPACE! FILL THIS SPACE!** Thank You for restoration. Father, I love, and I adore You. You have free reign here, so I give You back what is Yours, for I am Yours, and my house is Yours. All that I have belongs to You. Since You just entered this space, freedom will not just be an appearance, but it will be my resting place in Jesus' name. AMEN!!!

Chapter 6: The Return

Restored: return (someone or something) to
a former condition, place, or position.

The spirit of the Lord says to you: **"I've given you the grace to be pure again."** The purity before the rape, molestation, word curses, rejection, homosexuality, loneliness, brokenness, bitterness, low self-esteem, and un-forgiveness, is the purity that God desires to restore back to you. However, we look at purity as being fragile, so we think that once something has been tainted it can no longer be pure, but God's presence will always make us clean again.

After being entangled in perversion for so long, it begins to cover your identity and many of you, like me, have been submerged in perversion. My identity was literally ripped from me in elementary school, so I had pretty much gone my entire life without knowing who I really was. Contrarily, there is a grace that God released to me, and even now He is releasing it to you. It is a grace that uncovers identity no matter how long it has been buried. His truth restores purity. Even now, I prophesy that the blinders the enemy had on you are falling off. You will experience a season of being replenished and refreshed. I see the Lord blowing the residue and debris off the lives of those who desire His freedom. If you allow God to clean you, it does not have to take ten years. In a matter of weeks, He can free you from everything that opposes His will for your life. He restored me in this very manner, and all I had to do was initiate and truly decide I no longer wanted any parts of what I had been in for so long. I surrendered my past but also my future. He then began to deal with that which held me in bondage. He had me to face everything that truly caused me to walk away from Him. Transparently, I dealt with the why, who, what, and the me. I had to come out of agreement with the word curses spoken over me, and I also dealt with what drew me to pornography, masturbation, and homosexuality, so you must do the same. I opened up to God in such a way that He became my private journal, and everything I felt I released to Him. He took what I gave Him and worked with me. He rid me of even my perverted perception of myself and showed me my worth. Every chain the enemy has wrapped around you is a lie, and you unravel those chains with God's truth concerning you. I can tell you truthfully today that I desire nothing that the enemy has to offer because I understand truth.

God's Truth = Your Purity. If you want purity, put on God's truth.

God will restore masculinity, femininity, and anything else you lack. There is no limit to what our Father will do to restore His children.

May your season of staleness and stagnation be cut short. May every demonic power that desires to keep you be cut up and sent to dry places. I loose you from the grip of hell. Rise and take your rightful place as children of the Most-High God!

I want to encourage you that the blood of Jesus WILL restore you! Despite how many times you tell God that you are sorry, and this is the last time, even when you returned just to do it all again, God will restore you. No matter how many altar calls you went to or how as soon as you left the altar you gave in to your flesh again, God will restore you. Even after all of this still, you cannot out sin God's grace.

He is waiting with His arms wide open. Jesus went to the cross to give you the opportunity to be pure/clean. Even when we have abused the cross and the purpose of it over and over, Jesus would do it all again an infinite amount of times. I learned this firsthand; I am living proof! What is even more amazing is that as we continue to walk through this deliverance process, God's grace will not only cover you, but it will wash you, and no residue will remain. I declare that you will not even look like what you have been through.

The only way people will know what you have been through is if you opened your mouth to tell them. Jesus came that we may have life and life more abundantly *(John 10:10)*.

It's because of Him that we have an opportunity to live a completely free life. His grace is tangible, and it came here into the Earth just for you! This chapter does not require you to do much.

The moment you create a space for God to dwell in your life again is the moment you reopen the door for purity.

If you listen as the Holy Spirit leads, you will slowly but surely walk into complete freedom. I have come to learn that purity is posture-based. If you follow all the strategies released in this book and posture yourself correctly, you will set yourself up for The Return!

Declare This: I HAVE THE GRACE TO BE PURE AGAIN!!!

Purity is returning to every area of my life:

- My Mind is pure!

- My Heart is pure!

- My Vision is pure!

- My Will is pure!

- My Desires are pure!

- My Actions are pure!

- My Dreams are pure!

- My Motives are pure!

- My Body is a temple FULL of the presence of God!

- My Bloodline is pure!

- My Relationships are pure!

- My Sexual desires are pure! (There is such a thing as pure sexual desire which comes from God). In the matchless name of Jesus, Amen!!!

PTTKM Workbook Chapter 6 – The Return

1) After reading this chapter, how would you define *grace*?

_____

_____

_____

2) Have you made the proper adjustments in your life to experience a restoration of purity?

_____

_____

_____

_____

3) If no, what is the hold up? If yes, how are you feeling, and what have you changed?

_____

_____

_____

_____

_____

Strategic Prayer – The Return

Father, thank You for loving me. Thank You that I am not too dirty to experience Your grace, no matter what I did or how long I did it, or when I stopped doing it. You are not consumed with unimportant details, but You care about me. Thank You for loving me despite me and thank You for love that heals me and makes me whole. I do not deserve Your grace, but You freely give it to me. I do not deserve Your mercies, but they are new every single morning.

Lamentations 3:22-23 asserts (NLT): "The steadfast love of the Lord never ceases; his mercies never come to an end; they are new every morning; great is your faithfulness."

I am so glad that You reached way down and picked me up as filthy as I was; I love You for that. Father, thank You for the grace You have released to me, the grace to be pure again and grace that unleashes my identity. Not only did You preserve me, but You washed me. I am grateful that I do not look like what You brought me out of. Thank You for removing the residue. Thank You that every mark of the enemy is gone. Thank You for the price You paid for me before I was even a thought. Thank You for releasing grace before I ever needed it! Thank You for Your blood that washes me white as snow. I will walk in the purity that the blood of Jesus has paid for, so my fate is sealed, and my purity is evident. Freedom will not just be an appearance, but it will be my resting place in Jesus' name. Amen!!!

Chapter 7: Book of Prayers

Legal Rights/Legal Ground

A *legal right/legal ground* is something that gives a spirit/ demon the opportunity to enter or continue to harass us. It gives them the right to remain within us, even when we try to cast them out or remove the cycles that come with them from our lives.

Types of Legal Rights

Sins
- Willful and un-repented

Soul Ties
- Ungodly

Demonic Vows or Oaths
- Demonic commitments (i.e. verbal agreements that tie your soul to anything that opposes God)

Un-forgiveness
- You must forgive yourself along with anyone who could have possibly hurt you. Your freedom depends on your willingness to forgive, so un-forgiveness can literally block you from freedom.

Ancestral Sins
- Generational curses or cycles (that have yet to be broken)

Traumatic Experiences or Events
- Rape or molestation (can open the door for continued torment, causing a stronghold to be formed in your mind, if not dealt with properly)

Word Curses
- Your words or the words of others spoken over you could keep doors to continued demonic harassment open.

Occult Involvement (Of any kind): A few of the most popular involvements include but are not limited to:
- Palm Readings, Occult Games, Astrology
- Psychic Readings, Tarot Cards, Horoscopes
- Witchcraft, Voodoo, The Invocation of Evil Spirits

Accursed Objects and Symbols (Objects connected to evil spirits, sources, and/or false gods): A few of the most popular objects include but are not limited to:
- Amulets
- Talismans
- Good Luck Charms
- Enchanted Objects (e.g. Dreamcatchers)
- Idols (false gods, Golden calf)

Breaking Legal Rights:

- You must first forgive; un-forgiveness will keep you from receiving full deliverance.

- Release all ties with any demonic sources or powers, including getting rid of cursed objects or anything occult-related.

- Figure out what doors you have opened and what spirits you have given legal rights to.

- The next step is renunciations.

- Renounce any connections to evil spirits and repent.

- Get rid of anything that ties you back to perversion, such as erotic books.

Declare This: I break all contractual agreements and legal rights with any ungodly spirit I have been in connection with. I breach and forfeit all contracts. I sever every tie that keeps me connected to unclean spirits that would bind and trap me. I break these ties with the blood of Jesus and with the fire of God. I renounce all affiliation with every ungodly spirit in Jesus' name. Amen!!!

Prayer Against Spirit Of Perversion

Under the power of the only living God I break the bands of wickedness; I destroy the doors of bondage and I snatch my freedom! I declare that I cannot and will no longer be bound. Every snare, trap, plot and plan of Satan must bow at the name of Jesus. I remove the muzzle, and I call on the strong name of JESUS. I release the Lion of Judah to roar and shatter every demonic presence of perversion that has gripped me and my bloodline. You must come down now, and you must be destroyed now. Spirit of perversion I am no longer subject to your power; no longer am I subject to your grip. You must let me go! Let go of my mind, my will, my desires and attractions. I break every legal right that this spirit has to me, and I close every single door I have opened or even the doors family members have opened. I announce my emancipation NOW. I stand and decree I have legal right to freedom because the Father said so, and Jesus gave it to me. So now I command all perverse memories, and imaginations to be burned with fire. Rape and Molestation REMOVE your grip. No longer will I be bound by past traumatic experiences. Whatever was in the bloodline that released perversion, I stop your flow, and I cut you off in Jesus' name. I destroy generational curses caused by these demonic activities. Father cover my mind and remove demonic thinking. I declare that the progression of perversion has been halted and must come to an end. Father, THE destroyer of corrupt imaginations, restore purity to every part of my mind.

Forgive me for fulfilling my unclean desires. Deliver me from idolizing myself and my needs and wants. Wash me in Your blood Jesus. Thank You for grace to be pure again. Thank You for grace to be free, no matter what piece or side of perversion I was entangled in. I ask that You release angels on my behalf to fight for me and to help me get and STAY free. I refuse to continue to wrestle with my will and Your will for me. I release every tie and connection I had with this demonic spirit in Jesus' name. Amen!!!

Prayer Against Shame And Condemnation

Genesis 3:21 "Unto Adam also and to his wife did the Lord God make coats of skins, and clothed them."

This scripture is extremely significant to me because after their joint disobedience, which produced an awareness that they were naked causing shame to set in, God made provision to free them from even their self-inflicted shame. I declare today that you are fully clothed, and shame is not your portion. There is no reason to run and hide because our Father has already covered you from even the repercussions of what you've done.

Father, I thank You that after I've confessed and repented of my sin You do not hold on it, nor do You hold it over my head. It is not Your will that I be bound. It is not Your will for replays to consistently fill my mind and torment me. However, freedom is Your will for me. So, even now I pray Your will to be done. Help me walk in the freedom You have established for me, long before I was ever created to need it. I accept Your freedom for my life now. I choose this moment to walk in it. No longer will I feel the shame of what I did or what I did not do, or who I did it with or what was done to me. I thank You that Your son has made ME free. So, I rest in that even now. SHAME must fall off! Humiliation and condemnation be banished! You demonic tormenting oppressor, I break your power, and I destroy your kingdom. No longer will I be defeated; I rise as the giant whom God has called me to be. Beneath is not who I am.

Deuteronomy 28:13 "*And the LORD will make you the head and not the tail; you shall be above only, and not be beneath, if you heed the commandments of the LORD your God, which I command you today, and are careful to observe them.*" So, I speak from the seat of a son. No longer will I allow you to make me feel powerless or less than a son. No longer will I live as a peasant when God calls me Heir in Jesus' name. Amen!!!

Prayer for Personal Forgiveness

I acknowledge Jesus Christ as my personal Savior, and everything else before this moment does not matter. What I was previously entangled in does not matter because Jesus came so that life could be my portion, and I accept that portion now. No longer will I stay in self-made prisons, but I break out of the bondage of yesterday, and I step in the freedom of today. Regret is not and will never be my portion. I eradicate playbacks of past mistakes and memories of misery. Therefore, I release the healing oil of the Father to soothe every pain of my mistakes. I forgive myself because God has already forgiven me. I am a new creature, and my past will not distort my future because I am NEW. I decree it in Jesus' name. ***Romans 8:1 promises: "There is therefore now no condemnation to them which are in Christ Jesus, who walk not after the flesh, but after the Spirit."*** So, Father, I thank You that shame has no place because I no longer walk in the flesh but after the spirit, so I am free. I forgive myself, and I cannot change what I have done, but no longer will I live in it. I walk out of the prison of my past now. No longer am I a slave; no longer am I in a hostage situation. Christ has come and delivered me freedom, so I walk in it. Every self-punishing spirit must go. I am not concerned with the opinions of others or what they know about me. I am concerned only with what the Father thinks about me. His word affirms me. I no longer walk in the flesh but after the spirit. Thank You, ABBA- Father.

Prayer For Emotional Healing

Father, I lay down every word people have spoken over or about me. I lay down my opinion of me, and I lay down every flaw I see in me. I pick up Your perception of me. I pick up the words You have spoken over me; I pick up Your opinion of me, and I pick up Your healing for me. Father, thank You that You see me as beautiful; as wonderfully made. You did not make me to be broken nor did You make me to be insignificant. However, You established me as royalty, so I remove comparison. I will stop looking at what people have that I do not, and I will recognize what You have given me! I thank You that I am loved and thank You for accepting me and seeing me as worthy. Even when I see myself to be worth nothing, You constantly tell me in Your Word whom I am, and I intentionally choose to allow those words to override any negative words or thoughts concerning me. Father, continue to destroy rejection. I remove any rejected mentality that I picked up. I speak to my self-esteem, and I tell it to rise because there is no way I can worship the Creator and not reverence what He created, including myself. Therefore, I acknowledge that I was not made; I was CREATED. You did not just whip me up, but every detail about me was patiently chosen. I walk in the knowledge of that in this very moment. I am healed, not broken. Emotional brokenness is not my portion. I am whole in every way, and I will no longer search for people's approval or validation. I will not search for validation or fill voids through sexual activity, masturbation, or pornography. I will not look to be accepted by homosexuality or any ungodly source. Wholeness is my portion. God is my source of validation and affirmation. You are the well that I will draw from forever. Let any idea that goes against this prayer be destroyed in Jesus' name. Let every void be filled now in Jesus' name. Amen!!!

Prayer For The Sexually Abused

Father remove the pain, bitterness, and shame that I have felt from being sexually abused. Deliver me from the tormenting flashbacks. Free me from all resentment. I know that in order to experience my full deliverance I must release this into Your hands. Help me to forgive my abuser or abusers. Help me to forgive those whom I expected to be there who were not. Help me to forgive every person who did not believe me. Help me to forgive every person who told me that there was something I could have done to prevent this. No longer will I blame myself. Father forgive me for the anger and bitterness I had toward You. Forgive me for feeling like this was Your fault or like You were not there. Father undo all the damage this has caused me mentally, emotionally, spiritually, physically, and even sexually. Father remove the residue of sexual trauma and even the fear of intimacy. Untie the soul of my abuser from me. Help me not to carry the trauma of sexual abuse into my marriage. Allow me to be open and feel safe with my spouse. I drop this baggage at Your feet; no longer do I desire to carry it. Father do away with it in Jesus' name! I release Your healing oil over my life. Heal every wound and crack. I take back everything that was stolen from me in Jesus' name. Give me unspeakable joy and peace that surpasses my understanding. I drop the weight of sexual abuse and torment. Burn it with fire in Jesus' name. Amen!!!

Prayer For The Sexual Abuser

Psalm 73:21-26 (KJV) reads: "Thus my heart was grieved, and I was pricked in my reins. So foolish was I, and ignorant: I was as a beast before thee. Nevertheless, I am continually with thee: thou hast holden me by my right hand. Thou shalt guide me with thy counsel, and afterward receive me to glory. Whom have I in heaven but thee? and there is none upon earth that I desire beside thee. My flesh and my heart faileth: but God is the strength of my heart, and my portion forever."

Father forgive me for allowing my desires to get the best of me and forgive me for making that impulsive decision that will forever affect someone's life. I pray that You settle their spirit and heart, for I cannot take back what I did, but You can make them whole again. Forgive me for defiling a temple that You created. Father, I ask that You wash me clean and that You kill the seed of lust that has caused me to act in such a way. Father restore the goods that I have so unrighteously stolen. Father, I ask that You not allow my sins to trickle down through generations after me. Shut the doors to perversion that I so foolishly operated in. Heal my inward parts. I do not want to continue to carry this. Despite what my mind tells me, I am loved and forgiven. Father remove the torment of guilt and condemnation from my mind. Father I need You to break off the power of the accuser of the brethren (Satan). I am not what I have done, and even after all I have done You still hold my hand. You

STILL call me Son (Not gender based). Father I am amazed at the fact that I'm still important to You. Thank You for not being like man. You could drop me, but You continue to hold me. I love You, and I am grateful. Remove any snare or trap that would make deliverance unreachable; clean and clear my mind from the flashbacks or even desires to do it again. Father, help me not to feel like I have fallen so far that I might as well continue in what I have been in. Nothing will drive me to this point ever again. Thank You that Your blood washes me clean. I will walk in the knowledge of my purity through Christ Jesus from this day on in Jesus' name. AMEN!!!

Prayer Against Pedophilia

Pedophilia is of the deepest levels of perversion because it is no longer fair ground. At the point in which the door to pedophilia is opened, the spirit of perversion begins to operate on a multigenerational level, much like molestation. Multiple generations are tormented the moment this door is opened.

Therefore, spirit of the living God, I repent for looking at children as anything other than what You originally designed them for. Take any lustful desire to pursue them away. Lord, I ask You to forgive me for allowing myself to be used as a gateway for the enemy to destroy the purity of generations. I ask that You wash me and clean my soul concerning how I view children and change my perception concerning Your creation. Please forgive me for my heathen-like ways. Rid me of the shame, guilt, and condemnation. Reveal the root of where this unholy desire began. Father allow me to face it, so it can be completely uprooted. Destroy this fetish by fire. Give me holy and pure sexual desires in Jesus' name. Amen!!!

Prayer Against Trauma

Father I come into Your presence now submitting all remnants of trauma that have attached themselves to me in previous seasons of my life. I desire that you would completely rip away any unhealed and unresolved wounds of the past that continue to affect my today and possibly my tomorrow. Remove all suffering connected to the spirit of perversion and sexual immorality. Father I ask that You heal the deep isolated parts of my soul, even the places that appear to be a mystery to me, because of the things I've knowingly and even unknowingly buried in my subconscious mind. My prayer is that all the debris that I have yet to fully release be removed, including the areas that I have tried to simply forget about and situations that I chose to pretend never occurred. Go down deep into those places and expose the wounds so that I can be healed. I no longer desire to be controlled by my past. I no longer desire to love based on my past. I no longer desire to live like old situations are going to keep repeating themselves. I no longer desire to repeat cycles. Father I don't know how to move forward on my own, so I call on Holy Spirit the helper. Father in this very moment give the strength to drop all of the baggage I've carried. I release now all childhood trauma. I release all trauma from my teenage years. I release all trauma that has or would attempt to follow me into adulthood. I release traumatic words that were spoken over me. I release every traumatic sexual encounter and experience I've had. I release all of the traumatic things I've done to myself. Under the power of Holy Spirit and the authority of Jesus Christ I command now that the power of trauma fail and be destroyed. May every demonic stronghold that has been set in place to bind me forever to those experiences be destroyed. May every stronghold in my life that stood in my mind crumble and fall to the ground. Father I pray now that You would remove the power that these experiences have had on my past, present and especially my future. Father I give You complete and total control of my mind, heart and soul. I ask now that You would cause proper alignment and healing to manifest in my life now. I am no longer prisoner to trauma, but I am free because the Son has made me free. I declare it to be so now in Jesus' name Amen!!!

Prayer Against Soul Ties

Father, I give You my mind, heart, and will. I ask that You wash my entire being, remove any ungodly thing that grips me. Untie any demonically charged soul tie from me. Rip my soul away from anything that desires to bind me. Devour that which desires to entangle my soul. Rip my soul from the soul of anyone whom I was never meant to be tied to. Help me untangle my heart, will, and mind from them. Untangle me sexually, emotionally, and mentally. May I become numb to their devices and ploys to continually keep me under their subjection. I cut the cords of this ungodly tie in Jesus' name. I pick up my individuality and my identity in You. I receive Your wholeness for my life. Never again will I be divided between whom I choose to serve. No longer will I make people my god or idol. Father help me shift my desires. Even as the deer pants for water, allow me to long for You in the same way. I need more of You. Father fill my every void with You. Give me a passion for You. I open the door for Godly and righteous soul ties. Knit my soul together with those whom You desire. I give You possession and complete control of me and all my members. I seal this prayer in Jesus' name. Amen!!!

Prayer Against Sexual Torment In Sleep

Belial - Satan, the embodiment of all that is evil and perverse. The one who has charge over perverse and seducing spirits, and sends them out for your personal torment.

Incubus - The male version of an evil spirit that has intercourse with women in their sleep, causing erotic fantasies, and continued perversion in their life. We are opened to these kinds of spirits the moment we open the door to perversion, and until it is properly shut, they have access to us.

Succubus - The female version of an evil spirit that has intercourse with men in their sleep, causing erotic fantasies, and continued perversion in their life. We are opened to these kinds of spirits the moment we open the door to perversion, and until it is properly shut, they have access to us.

Under the power of Holy Spirit, and in the authority of Jesus Christ, the true and living God, I decree that every unclean spirit that has taken my home as its dwelling place must go now. Father send Your angels to watch over me and war on my behalf. I loose angels to chase out every unclean spirit in my dwelling place. Father, I ask that You remove every demonic spirit that desires to find dwelling in my sleep. I speak to the mountain of Belial and command that it be crushed now in Jesus' name. I break the power of Belial. I break the power of every seducing spirit like Incubus and Succubus. To every unclean thought that causes or triggers erotic fantasy, GET OUT NOW! I bind loneliness- it will not cause me to fall. I break down the walls of sexual vulnerability, and I decree strength in my members. Father Your word says that "when I'm weak, You are strong" (**2 Corinthians 12:10**), so strength of the Lord come upon me now. **I AM VICTORIOUS!** I have already overcome, and I will not go back. I know that the agenda of the enemy who desires to kill me is to wrap up my sin in my humanity. I am human, but I will be holy, for you are holy (**1 Peter 1:16**). Now I speak over my sleep. I renounce wet dreams and sleep fantasies. Sexual demons cannot have me. Every Incubus and Succubus-like spirit is banished from THIS home- you are forbidden! You cannot have my mind, my sleep, or my body. Be driven out in Jesus' name with fire. I will rest, and even my dreams will be pure. Father make Your desires mine. Father allow it not to be a struggle to sleep from this night on, for I give my room back to You. Father, I say dwell and consume everything that is not like You in Jesus' name. AMEN!!!

Prayer Against Ungodly Sexual Desires

Father, in Jesus' name, I submit all my desires, including my sexual appetite, before You. I give You permission to destroy every sexual idol I have established in my mind. I declare that my mind will fall subject to the will of God. Every erotic visual, idea, and desire be banished now. Immoral sensual appetites be dismantled in Jesus' name. My mind has been transformed and renewed, and I will not go back. I will fight for holiness and purity. I crave to be in Your presence Father, because it is in Your presence that my voids are filled. Come and fill me like never before. Increase my appetite for You. Allow me to drink from Your well that never runs dry. It is at Your well that my desires are quenched and Your desires for me flourish. It is at Your well that strength comes upon me. So now, well of living water satisfy me; fill me until I want no more. Holy Spirit, I give You FULL permission to flood, to overtake, and to overwhelm my mind with Your presence. Father, I surrender my will. Let my thoughts line up with Your thoughts for me. I command my body to fall subject to the needs of the Father. I desire Your yoke, so yoke of the enemy be broken now. May mental bondage be broken. I bind the traps and snares of the enemy in Jesus' name. Hell, you have no territory here, for I AM property of the Most-High God! So now, I call down every voice other than the Father's, and I remove the power of wickedness. I will live HOLY. I will desire righteously; even my sexual desires will be holy in Jesus' name. AMEN!!!

Prayer Against Lust

Job 31:1 (GNT) asserts: "I have made a solemn promise never to look with lust at a woman."

Psalm 119:37 (NLT) commands: "Turn my eyes from worthless things and give me life through your word."

Matthew 5:28 (NLT) rebukes: "But I say, anyone who even looks at a woman with lust has already committed adultery with her in his heart."

Romans 8:6 (NIV) reminds "The mind governed by the flesh is death, but the mind governed by the Spirit is life and peace."

Father forgive my eye gates for what they have looked upon in days past. I ask that You wash me from all iniquity and lust. Father clean my vision. Give me covenant eyes because I want to see what You see. Change my vision and let me see You everywhere I look. Help me to see You more freshly and differently than I ever have before. I want to see You high and lifted up; lifted above my desires, thoughts, and imaginations. I bring every one of the members of my body under subjection now **(1 Corinthians 9:27)**. I declare freedom from impurity, and I see Your children as you see them. I will not look at them as targets, and I refuse to be a vicious predator by undressing everyone who is pleasing to the eye and seeing them as mere prey. Remove all demonic activity from my eyes and let them see You. Shut my eyes to the world and

84

let them see the kingdom of God. Lust has no place in me, so let it be driven out with fire now. Lustful desires and thoughts will not fill any of my members. Allow your presence to be what I desire to see in Jesus' name. AMEN!!!

Prayer Against Sexual Addictions

1 Corinthians 10:13-14

"13 No temptation has overtaken you except what is common to mankind. And God is faithful; he will not let you be tempted beyond what you can bear. But when you are tempted, he will also provide a way out so that you can endure it."

"14 Therefore, my dear friends, flee from idolatry."

Jesus, I surrender now every appetite that is not in Your will for me. I surrender to Your plan and design for my life. I bring to the altar of sacrifice every idol I have built and erected for my personal pleasures. I lay down every addiction and the routine that comes with them. I no longer desire to be controlled by cravings. Take away the continual craving of lust and perversion which are never satisfied. Jesus, it is my desire to be captive and slave to no one; even You give me the choice to serve You. Sexual addiction, however, seems to override my choices and my desires for purity. So, I now employ the helper, Holy Spirit, because there is no way I can fight this battle on my own. I need Your help completely. Father reroute me and remove all routines related to every sexual addiction I've been bound to. Father destroy even the cravings of previous sexual partners I may have been with. I ask that You completely destroy that which continues to bind me over and over. I exchange my addictions for Your freedom.

Father I ask that You give me Godly hobbies and productive activities to replace the idle time I've spent with idols. I want Your presence, which refines and refreshes, to come and enter me. Fill me until I am overflowing with Your precious spirit. I release every demonic burden and yoke from around my neck to You and I take on Your yoke and Your burden for my life. In Jesus name. Amen!!!

Prayer Of Repentance From Masturbation And Pornography

Psalm 51:1-19 (NLT) reads:

1 Have mercy on me, O God,
because of your unfailing love.

Because of your great compassion,
blot out the stain of my sins.

2 Wash me clean from my guilt.
Purify me from my sin.

3 For I recognize my rebellion;
it haunts me day and night.

4 Against you, and you alone, have I sinned;
I have done what is evil in your sight.

You will be proved right in what you say,
and your judgment against me is just.

5 For I was born a sinner—
yes, from the moment my mother conceived me.

6 But you desire honesty from the womb, teaching me
wisdom even there.

88

7 Purify me from my sins, and I will be clean;
wash me, and I will be whiter than snow.

8 Oh, give me back my joy again;
you have broken me—
now let me rejoice.

9 Don't keep looking at my sins.
Remove the stain of my guilt.

10 Create in me a clean heart, O God.

11 Do not banish me from your presence,
and don't take your Holy Spirit from me.

12 Restore to me the joy of your salvation,
and make me willing to obey you.

13 Then I will teach your ways to rebels,
and they will return to you.

14 Forgive me for shedding blood, O God who saves;
then I will joyfully sing of your forgiveness.

15 Unseal my lips, O Lord,
that my mouth may praise you.

16 You do not desire a sacrifice, or I would offer one.
You do not want a burnt offering.

17 The sacrifice you desire is a broken spirit.
You will not reject a broken and repentant heart, O God.

18 Look with favor on Zion and help her;
rebuild the walls of Jerusalem.

19 Then you will be pleased with sacrifices offered in the
right spirit— with burnt offerings and whole burnt
offerings.
Then bulls will again be sacrificed on your altar.

Father, I do not even feel worthy to talk to You right now. I feel like You are sick and tired of me saying I am sorry and then going back and doing the same thing. Despite my feelings, here I am again, and somewhere deep down in the back of my mind, I know You are still listening, so here I am. I do not want to keep being in this same situation time after time, week after week, day after day. I admit that without You I am stuck, and I completely admit that I do not know how to get out of this alone. I do not want to be here, but I find myself feeling as if I cannot move. I feel weak. Although I am weak, I am grateful that Your word says that when I am weak You are strong, so Father stand up in me. Help me to choose Your will over mine. I give You permission to override my will because sometimes I do not have enough strength to choose You.

Father forgive me for not listening to good judgement or counsel. Holy Spirit, please do not take Your voice from my often-shut ear. Help me to open my ears and hear You again and listen; give me strategy to resist my flesh. Father forgive me for treating Your grace like a revolving door-like I can just walk in and out when I choose. I am sorry that I have taken the blood of Jesus for granted. Clean me again and do whatever it takes to shake me out of this place. Free me from pornography; free me from masturbation, and free me from using my hands or fingers to fill voids. Forgive me for using my ears to hear anything other than Your voice. Forgive me for using my imagination for sexual fantasies. Forgive me for spilling precious seed to the ground. Forgive me for feeling like the only way I can feel better is by taking part in these demonic activities. Help me to lean on You. You are the remedy! Help me get up from this nasty soiled place. I NEVER want to return to such a place again. I want to run after You, so remove anything that makes it hard for me to do that. I desire to stop using masturbation and/or pornography as a coping mechanism. No longer will stress, depression, or even natural sexual desires lead to me returning to this dead place. I accept Your forgiveness for me in Jesus' name. Amen!!!

Prayer For Spouse Struggling With Pornography Addiction

Father, I give You complete control over my household and my marriage. Before I ask You to deal with my spouse, I ask that You deal with me. Help me to be understanding and long-suffering concerning everything they are dealing with. Father, I ask that You teach me how to maneuver between their boundaries to help them experience the freedom You have destined for their life before the foundation of the world. Father break every chain and cycle from their past and uproot every addiction they have succumbed to. Father use me to destroy the plans of the enemy concerning their life and destroy generational curses concerning our family. May Your spirit rise in my spouse and completely override any desires of their flesh. Knit our souls together and may we be sexually woven together and find pleasure in one another. Allow our love to completely take the desire for pornography away. Redeem our marriage in Jesus' name. Amen!!!

Prayer Against Generational Curses

Father, I thank You that I am engrafted into Your bloodline. I am grateful that You are the makeup of my DNA. Because I am your SON, I accept what **John 1:12 declares:** ***"But as many as received him, to them gave the power to become the sons of God, even to them that believe on his name."*** I am attached to You, so even now I speak to everything that is unjustly attached to me, and I break it off at the root. I destroy and shatter generational curses, hexes, spells, and vows, and I erase and eradicate all demonic agreements my forefathers made. Father, I stand in the gap for my family saying forgive us of any unrighteous act we have committed. Father, I go back ten generations asking You to forgive us for the things we have done both knowingly and unknowingly. Father forgive us for having anything to do with the occult and forgive us for opening any doors to witchcraft by reading horoscopes, going to psychics, doing palm readings, and pledging our allegiance to anything other than You. Remove us from any entanglement and snares of demonic influences from those we know and even those we do not know that are attached to our family. Forgive us for opening the door to any presence or any source other than You. You are our strong redeemer. I break off all ancestral struggles, so I declare that what my parents, their parents, and their parents' parents went through and struggled with is NOT, and never will be my portion. I am the healed of God and the freed of God. In this very moment, I call forth the breaker to loose the shackles of poverty and sexual perversion and to abolish addictions to drugs and alcohol. I demand spirits of rejection, anger, murder, bitterness, low self-esteem, worry, stress, bondage, incest, homosexuality, whoremongering, early age death, and inherited sickness of any sort be removed. (Call the ones in your family out)!!! I declare in the name of Jesus that these spirits come OUT, and I send them to dry places. I remove the spirit of fear. We are MORE than conquerors, so we will eat the good of the land. We WILL see the salvation of the Lord. I decree that my family has been hidden in the blood of Jesus, so every demonic cycle must pass over because of the blood. Abba, thank You that the powers of darkness are no match for You, the only true and living GOD. Amen!!!

Prayer Against Premature Sexual Curiosity & Perverse Attachments For Children

Father, I come now asking that You would cover my children, nieces, nephews, and any young children or young adults connected to me. I ask that You establish a hedge of protection around them and that You would allow no demonically charged influences and no perverted plans or schemes to attach themselves to my children. I ask that You cover them from perverted spirits and experiences, and I ask that You cover them from predators or anyone with an impure agenda concerning them. I ask that You assist me in censoring what I allow them to see. I ask that You heighten my spiritual awareness to know what is going on in their personal lives, even at school or work. Father show me how to cover my children, nieces, nephews, and other youth. Show me how to be a good example of purity for them and allow me to see any perverted doors that I have opened that could possibly affect them. Let my eyes be opened to see the real and the fake concerning them. Father cover their ears and cover their eyes and let nothing unclean enter their spirits. Allow me to never be off watch. I ask that You cover them from homosexuality, and I ask that You cover them from lesbianism, promiscuity, whoremongering, and sexual addictions like pornography and masturbation. Cover them from door-opener spirits like rejection and depression. Do not allow suicidal thoughts or matters of demonic powers to leech onto them. Cover them from even the things I was exposed to. I renounce every ungodly door I have opened, and I break all ties and agreements with any demonic spirit or source. I ask that the sins of their forefathers would NOT trickle down to them, but You allow me to stand in position to break it at the root. I shatter and abolish ALL generational curses that have been waiting to leech on to them. I even go back to their birth, and I remove the things they were even born into, and I declare it will not sprout up in Jesus' name. I release generational blessings that have been held up to be released on them. Father be in their friendships and allow them to have Godly influences. Father allow them not to be emotionally broken causing them to attempt to fill voids that only You can fill. Help me to love them like You love the church. Help me cover them, teach them, and lead them. Father if there be any entanglement with the spirit of perversion in anyway, untangle them now Jesus' name. AMEN!!!

Prayer Against The Orphan Spirit

Galatians 3:26
For you are all sons of God through faith in Christ Jesus.

2 Corinthians 6:18
"And I will be a father to you, and you shall be sons and daughters to Me," Says the Lord Almighty.

Thank You, Father, for choosing me. Your word declares that we didn't choose You, but it's You who chose us. You've chosen me no matter what others have to say about it. You've chosen me in the face of my accusers. You choose me even when I'm not the popular choice.

Matthew 18:12-13
"How think ye? if a man have an hundred sheep, and one of them be gone astray, doth he not leave the ninety and nine, and goeth into the mountains, and seeketh that which is gone astray? And if so be that he find it, verily I say unto you, he rejoiceth more of that sheep, than of the ninety and nine which went not astray."

You choose me when I don't look the part, feel the part or act the part. When You see me, You see Your DNA, the work of Your hand and the fruit of Your labor. You see me as Your seed; as Your Son/Daughter. So, I dismantle the notion that I am an orphan. I dismantle the ideology that says I'm less than Your child. I break the power that the spirit of rejection has had over me and I command now that the spirit of the orphan be destroyed over my life. For You love me with an everlasting love which can be compared to anything in the Earth. Even when I was fully submerged in sin, You never disowned me. In fact, Your word says that You are married to the back sliders. I have not, nor will I ever be abandoned by You. Thank You for Your lavish love toward me. I accept the fullness of it now in Jesus name. Amen!!!

Prayer Against The Spirit Of The Harlot

Father forgive me for seeing myself through the lenses of perversion, for not seeing my true worth, and for pouring myself out to anyone who would receive me. I repent for every time I sold pieces of myself to the highest bidder when You see me as priceless. The price You paid for me will forever be unmatched. I repent for giving away something I didn't even buy, for I am not my own. At this very moment I call back to me all the parts of me that I've passed out and given to people. No longer will I settle in dysfunction. I lay down my many lovers to love You wholly. Forgive me for devaluing the work of art that I am. I repent for allowing people to use me, (Your temple) to do whatever they see fit. Your word declares that I am fearfully and wonderfully made. So, I call back even the years I poured out to people who used me up and then threw me away when they got what they needed from me. I call back the emotions I poured into people who didn't deserve my vulnerability. I will not be numb to true Godly love; instead, I will be ready. Father teach me how to wait on You for who You've created for me. No longer will I settle for what's available, but God give me Your will for my life. I renounce every word curse I've spoken over my own life and relationships. I am not a player and I am not a whore. I am a healed Son/Daughter. So, I renounce and release the connection to the spirit of the Harlot & The whoremonger.

Prayer To Be Hidden By The Blood Of Jesus

Father, even as I continue to walk out my daily deliverance process, I ask that You remove any residue of the filthy activities I was involved in or thought about. Wash me with Your precious blood and let all my sins and mistakes be hidden in the blood of Jesus. Let all my failures and flaws be hidden in the blood. Let all my weaknesses and past attractions be hidden in the blood. Father allow my testimony to be heard not seen due to me still carrying pieces of it. Restore my purity. Wash my mind, and let my thoughts be different. Purify my mind, and remove the dirty thoughts, visuals, and dirty activities I participated in. Remove every ungodly memory, even from my subconscious mind, and let me not be reminded of the way I chose to live before. Remove the guilt and shame and let me walk free from the bondage of the past. Let everything I used to do become foreign to me and let me get so wrapped up in you that the people I used to do things with cannot even recognize me. Hide me in Your blood until my mannerisms change, until my dialogue changes, until my desires change, and until every unrighteous thing connected to me is eradicated in Jesus' name. Let there be no trace of me when the enemy of my soul comes to look for me. In Jesus' name. Amen!!!

Prayer To Overcome The Power And Effects Of Homosexuality

Father, thank You for loving me. Thank You for calling me Son. Thank You for calling me "MAN". Thank You for giving me authority and dominion over the Earth just like You gave Adam. My words hold power and weight and what I speak must manifest. I speak that I am returning to Your original design and desire for my life. I pray now that You restore any level of masculinity that I feel I lack and help me to be confident in who You have called me to be as a man and a leader. Thank You for the power to be decide; I've decided that I do not have to go back to any lifestyle I was involved in, including homosexuality. No longer can strongholds and traumatic experiences like molestation, or rape, or the lack of my father or mother continue to bind me to ungodly lifestyles. I release now every name and word curses people have spoken over me. Remove any parts of low self-esteem that make me feel like I'm not worthy of the affection of a woman. My future is secured. Shame won't trick me out of my future. I speak to the future me now! I declare you are whole, and you are free, and no devil in Hell can bind you to who you used to be. Freedom is my portion and I will endure this journey as a good solider. I will not give up because it's easy to go back to the old lifestyle, but I will fight for my freedom.

Galatians 5:1 Stand fast therefore in the liberty wherewith Christ hath made us free and be not entangled again with the yoke of bondage.

May any other unclean, perverse spirit or attribute or mannerisms of Satan that I was exposed to be destroyed. Father, You have given me self-control, so help me to use it and grow it to resist the wiles of the enemy. Father take away the taste of that which is forbidden and give me holy desires. Holy Spirit, I need Your help. I cannot do anything without You. I will not try and fight the power of perversion without You. However, I will lean into Your strength for me, and I will win this battle now in Jesus name. Amen!!!!

Prayer To Overcome The Power And Effects Of Lesbianism

Father, thank You for loving me. Thank You for calling me Daughter. Thank You for calling me "WOMAN". Thank You for Your original desire and design for my life. Father I ask today that You remove any obstacle that makes Your original design and desire for my life difficult to believe. You have given me the assignment to labor alongside "MAN" and to bear much fruit. The enemy would see to it that I be off post and out of Your will, because He knows the power of agreement between "MAN" and "WOMAN" is unmatched and is God's perfect will concerning the two. Father I ask now that You would remove the scales from my eyes and show me the importance of the holy union. Remove any emotional wounds and scars that caused me to question or shift my sexuality because of previous traumatic circumstances like rape or molestation, the absence of or abuse of my father, the absence of a mother or the confusion of womanhood. Remove any feeling of shame or unworthiness that has made me feel unworthy of love from a Man after Gods heart. Help me realize just how fearfully and wonderfully made I really am. Allow me to experience a wholeness and completion in You like I have never experienced before. Free me from comparison and allow me to love myself completely. Father help me to remember I do not have to search for anybody's validation. Father break the power of any perverse spirit and allow purity to be my portion in Jesus' name. Amen!!!

Prayer To Flee Temptation

James 4:7 "Submit yourselves therefore to God. Resist the devil, and he will flee from you."

James 1:12 "Blessed is the man that endureth temptation: for when he is tried, he shall receive the crown of life, which the Lord hath promised to them that love him."

Father help me to realize that the presence of temptation is not the absence of purity, but a test of purity. In the past I have failed these tests miserably, but with Your power which lives on the inside of me and with the strategy in Your word, I can pass every single time. My prayer today is not that You would remove the temptation, but that You would give me strength to endure. I don't desire winning streaks which last for a moment and then eventually are swallowed up by defeat, but I'm after longevity and endurance. Father teach me how to endure and be sober in all decisions. I bind the power of demonically charged, impulsive decisions. I loose Your peace and Your strength, that I may endure through every level of temptation. Father I even thank You that temptation is only for a little while, but Your freedom is forever. Amen!!!

Prayer To Restore Sexuality

Father, I thank You for Your set order, for Your original plan, and for Your desire that a man be with a woman, and that is the only way. Your Word has asked us to be fruitful and multiply, and Satan knows that Your will cannot be made manifest with same-sex marriages and sexually immoral relationships. It is Satan's plan that Your will fail and that Your people be cut off, and he wants to use me for his plan. But I thank You that I am redeemed by You, Father. Step in and save me from myself. It is in my nature to do the opposite of Your will, so Father I ask for Your assistance in completing Your will and plan for my life. I lay down my old desires and fleshly ways. I pick up Your will for me, and I ask that You transform even my desires, transform my will, and transform what I am attracted to. If there be one, allow me to find that one You have predestined for me and remove demonic passions and attractions. Remove perverted sexual desires and remove memories of being with the same sex or desires of being with the same sex. Remove the way it made me feel or the imagination of the what it would make me feel like. Allow me to be pleased with whom You designed for me. Destroy the residue of any ungodly relationship I was in. Make me new. Father restore my sexuality to Your original design. Father I desire to be restored to who You ordained for me to be long before I entered the Earth. Father make me whole in my singleness and let me be staffed with those You've called me to for total transformation. In Jesus' name. Amen!!!

Prayer For Holiness

1 peter 1:16

for it is written: "Be holy, because I am holy."

Holy- dedicated or consecrated to God for a specific purpose; sacred, set apart.

Father Your word not only gives me a command to be holy, but it affirms the fact that it is possible for me to be holy. Teach me Your ways. Make me fit to be in Your glory. Make me fit to carry Your glory. Allow me to never be without Your glory. Allow me not to fall into the traps of the enemy causing my oil to be contaminated and my spirit exposed. Cover and cleanse me. Seal me in Your blood. Wash and purge me. I want to walk, do, and be all that You have set before me. Restore what has been taken, heal what was once broken, and cover what was exposed. May a Holy fire break out on the inside of me and consume that which is not pleasing to You. Father, even now, release the spirit of holiness. May a deep cry and yearning for holiness be birthed on the inside of me. May holiness be my passion and pursuit. Let Your glory fall on me like rain. Allow the fruit of being in Your glory to be holiness. I arise and take my rightful place as son. I desire to be holy because You, my Father, are holy. Allow me to be set apart specifically for your use. For so long I allowed everything else to use me, but it is my prayer that You alone use me. Let me be sacred and set apart; not perfect, but holy. It is so in Jesus' name. Amen!!!

Prayer To Welcome Holy Spirit Into Your Life

Psalm 84:10 "One day in your temple is better than a thousand anywhere else. I would rather serve in your house, than live in the homes of the wicked" (CEV).

Father Your word declares that better is one day in Your presence, than a thousand days anywhere else. Father forgive me for searching for better places and presences to be in, for every other court is a waste of my time. Every other court will surely fail but Yours will stand forever. I've been starving for Your presence. I long to have Your presence completely overtake & consume me. Sweet, Holy Spirit, I give You total permission to invade every nook and cranny of my life. Holy Spirit, I give You permission to be the loudest voice in my life. I thank You for Your spirit that advises and gives sound instruction; Your spirit that leads me into all truth. Holy Spirit fill me like never before. I've lived without You long enough, so with every fiber of my being I cry out "DWELL". As You dwell let every unclean thing fall off me in Your presence. King of glory let Your presence be released on and in me. My prayer is to never again feel far away from You. *Psalm 16:11 declares "You make known to me the path of life; in your presence there is fullness of joy; at your right hand are pleasures forevermore".* For everything I need is locked up in Your presence. The longevity of my deliverance is based on my proximity to You, hold me tight. Fill my home, car, workspace and my life. Let Your presence go with me all the days of my life in Jesus name. Amen!!!

Confession Of Forgiveness

Matthew 6:14-15
"For if ye forgive men their trespasses, your heavenly
Father will also forgive you: But if ye forgive not men
their trespasses, neither will your Father forgive your
trespasses."

This day I desire to be untied and untangled from the power
of bitterness and un-forgiveness. I
forgive_____ for

_____

_____

_____.

I don't desire to be held in bondage by the mistakes of men.
I desire to be a slave to nothing and no one. I desire that
you have that same freedom, so today I release you from
the prisons my bitterness created for you. I pray that the
same grace God has for me reaches you. I pray that peace is
your portion. Today, _____/_____/_____, I release you. In
Jesus name. Amen!!!

Signature x_____

Prayer Of Redemption

Lamentations 3:57-58

57 You came near when I called you, and you said, "Do not fear." 58 You, Lord, took up my case; you redeemed my life.

Isaiah 44:22 I have swept away your offenses like a cloud, your sins like the morning mist. Return to me, for I have redeemed you."

Ephesians 1:7 In him we have redemption through his blood, the forgiveness of sins, in accordance with the riches of God's grace.

Hebrews 10:10 Our sins are washed away and we are made clean because Christ gave His own body as a gift to God. He did this once for all time.

Father I thank You for Your grace, which is much like the ocean- its depths have yet to be discovered. And just when I thought I had reached my limit, You've shown me that Your grace is deeper than I could ever imagine. Thank You for thinking enough of me to not leave me to drown in my sin, but You've allowed me to sink into Your grace. Father I thank You for the beautiful thoughts You think of me, which far outnumber the grains of sand. Thank You for Your Son, and sacrifice, Jesus the resurrected one, who died so that I might meet Him in paradise. Thank You for your blood, Jesus. Thank You for being the complete and total atonement for sin, a debt I could never repay. Thank

You for Your rescuing power. Even when I am like a dog and decide to return to my own vomit, Your blood knows just how to find me. Your redemption power is limitless. The range of Your blood is endless. Thank You, Jesus, that every time I've called You, You've answered without hesitation. No longer will I allow what I've already been redeemed from to bind me. From this day forward I choose to live in the power of Your redemption. Not only have You redeemed me from sin & death, but You're also redeeming the time I've lost making poor decision and living a life that wasn't fruitful to who You've purposed for me to be in the Earth. I decree now that every harvest that was swallowed up by the locust due to my negligence, I will see again double fold. Father now I ask that not only would You give me the grace to snap back, but that it be released to my entire bloodline. Today I decide to resubmit to the redeemer and as a result of my submission I will lack no thing that was intended for me. In Jesus name. Amen!!!

Personal Prayer & Confession

Below, I want you to write your own personalized prayer to your specific issues, desires and needs. Don't be ashamed or afraid, this is completely between you and God.

_____

_____

_____

_____

_____

_____

_____

_____

_____

_____

_____

_____

_____

_____

_____

12 STEPS TO FREEDOM: Compiled List Of Strategies

1) Figure out why and how perversion entered your life.

2) Close the door to perversion.

   *Remove anything that makes this process difficult. *

3) Find what YOUR boundaries are. What makes you return to old habits?

*You may not be able to take what everyone else can take, and that is okay. It does not mean that you are weak. *

4) Forgive yourself!

5) Open doors of purity and allow people in who provoke continued deliverance into your life. Find accountability partners and be accountable to yourself, your partners, your family, and your leaders.

6) Submit your desires before God and pick up His desire for your life.

7) Retrain and renew your mind to think with the mind of Christ.

8) Walk in the spirit. Galatians 5:16 commands: "This I say then, walk in the Spirit, and ye shall not fulfill

the lust of the flesh."

9) Be TRANSPARENT 100% of the time. Deliverance comes alive in transparency.

10) PRAY!!! Prayer/Communion with ABBA is the most important part of deliverance because it keeps and covers you. You must develop a love for prayer if you want to stay delivered.

11) FAST!!!! The word of God declares in *Matthew 17:21 "Howbeit, this kind goeth not out but by prayer and FASTING"* There are some strongholds, and demonic attachments that only break with proper obedience and submission.

12) JESUS is the ultimate helper!!!!! Please understand that you are not saved by your own works, but by the perfected love of Jesus Christ. Lean into the strength that He provides! Trying to be saved on your own without the help of the blood & Holy Spirit will never work.

Be Free and Stay Free, in Jesus' Name!

For any further questions concerning the book and deliverance tips please feel free to contact me at: *jdh3ministries@gmail.com*